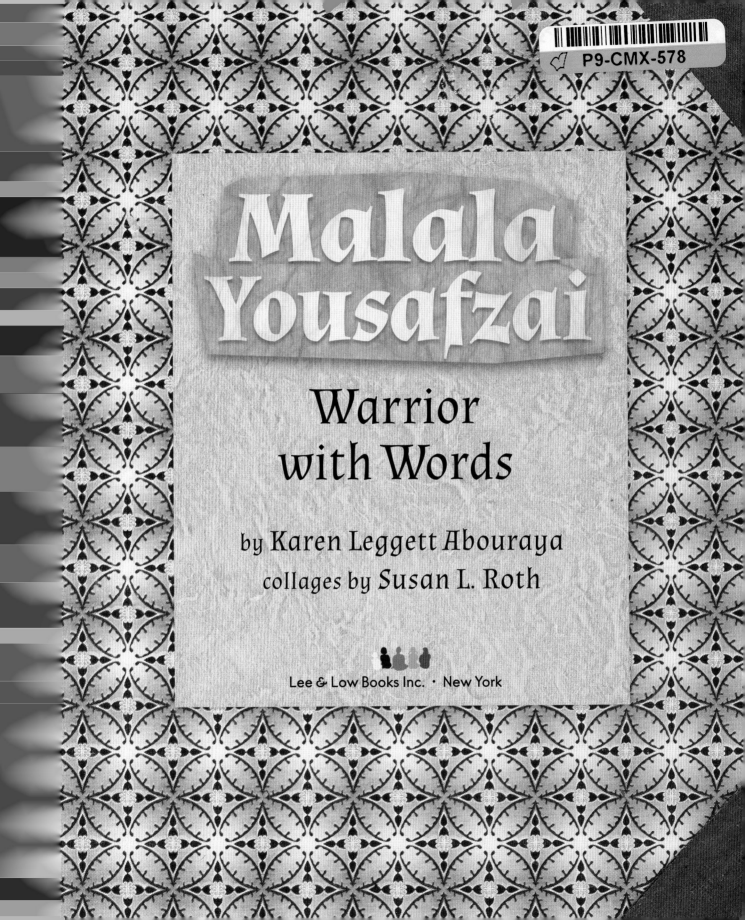

# Malala Yousafzai

## Warrior with Words

by Karen Leggett Abouraya

collages by Susan L. Roth

Lee & Low Books Inc. • New York

Acknowledgments

Our sincere appreciation to the scholars who reviewed versions of this manuscript, including: Aamina Shaikh and Sanaa Anwar from The Bridge Initiative, Prince Alwaleed Bin Talala Center for Muslim-Christian Understanding, Georgetown University; and Akbar Ahmed, Ibn Khaldun Chair of Islamic Studies, School of International Service, American University and former Pakistani High Commissioner to the UK and Ireland.　　　　　*—K.L.A.* and *S.L.R.*

Originally published as an e-book by StarWalk Kids Media

Redesign by David and Susan Neuhaus/NeuStudio
Production by The Kids at Our House
The text is set in Martin Gothic
The illustrations are rendered in paper and fabric collage
Manufactured in China by Jade Productions
Printed on paper from responsible sources
HC 10 9 8 7 6 5 4 3 2 1
PBK 10 9 8 7 6 5 4 3 2 1
First Lee & Low Books Edition 2019

Library of Congress Cataloging-in-Publication Data
Names: Abouraya, Karen Leggett, author. | Roth, Susan L., illustrator.
Title: Malala Yousafzai : warrior with words / by Karen Leggett Abouraya ; collages by Susan L. Roth.
Description: First Lee & Low Books edition | New York : Lee & Low Books Inc., 2019. | "Originally published as an e-book by StarWalk Kids Media." | Includes bibliographical references.
Identifiers: LCCN 2018016316 | ISBN 9781620147993 (pbk. : alk. paper) | ISBN 9781620148389 (hardcover : alk. paper)
Subjects: LCSH: Yousafzai, Malala, 1997—Juvenile literature. | Young women—Education—Pakistan—Biography—Juvenile literature. | Children's rights—Pakistan—Juvenile literature.
Classification: LCC LC2330 .A26 2018 | DDC 371.822095491—dc23
LC record available at https://lccn.loc.gov/2018016316

To my mother, Jean Leggett, for her unshakable dedication
to education, for herself, her children, and her students
—*K.L.A.*

For J.B. and N.P.
—*S.L.R.*

Malala Yousafzai is a warrior with words.
And Malala was a miracle in pink as she celebrated her sixteenth birthday. She did not have a sleepover. She celebrated by standing up for a cause. Malala was recovering from a serious injury. It was a miracle that she could stand at all. But she stood up in front of the whole world to prove that words have power.

In July 2013, Malala spoke in front of hundreds of young people and world leaders gathered at the United Nations in New York.

"We will bring change through our voice," she said. She asked every nation to make it possible for all children to go to school and live in peace.

Every country.

All children.

In peace.

"Our words can change the world," Malala said.

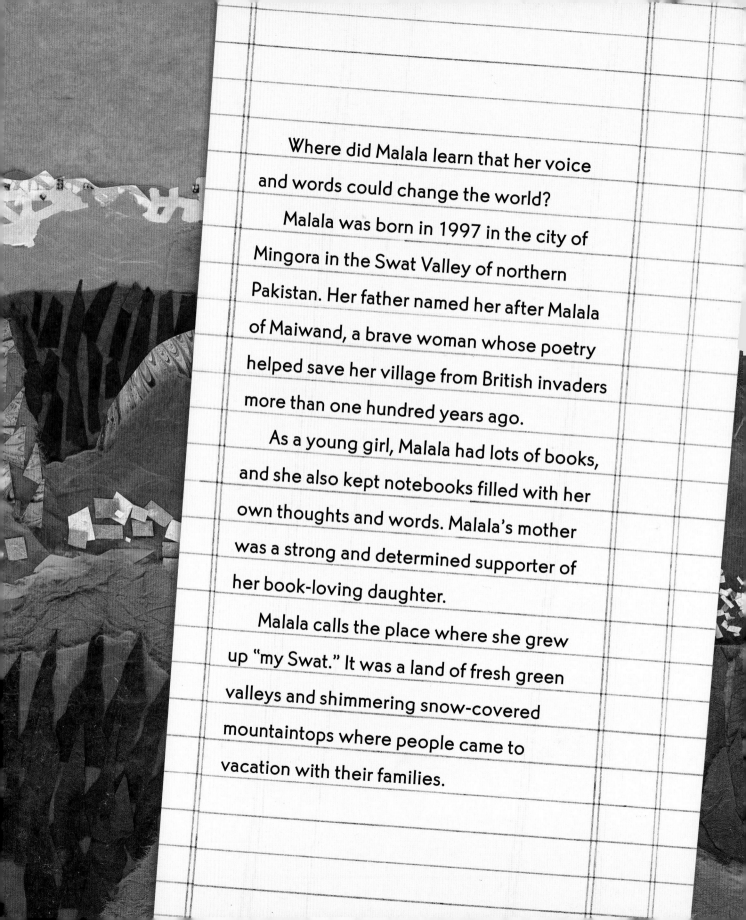

Where did Malala learn that her voice and words could change the world?

Malala was born in 1997 in the city of Mingora in the Swat Valley of northern Pakistan. Her father named her after Malala of Maiwand, a brave woman whose poetry helped save her village from British invaders more than one hundred years ago.

As a young girl, Malala had lots of books, and she also kept notebooks filled with her own thoughts and words. Malala's mother was a strong and determined supporter of her book-loving daughter.

Malala calls the place where she grew up "my Swat." It was a land of fresh green valleys and shimmering snow-covered mountaintops where people came to vacation with their families.

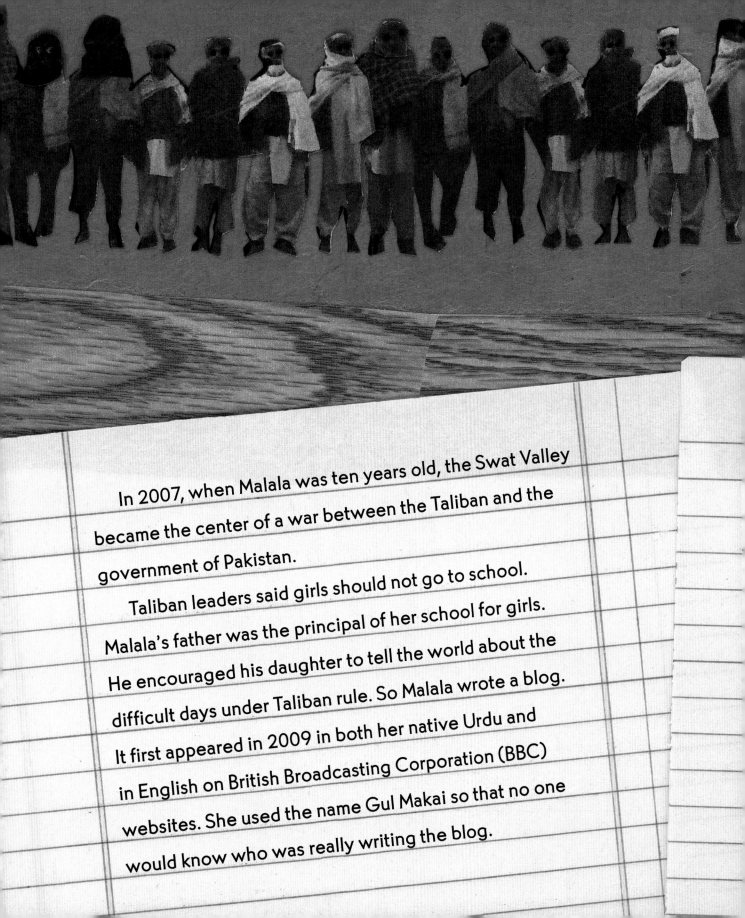

In 2007, when Malala was ten years old, the Swat Valley became the center of a war between the Taliban and the government of Pakistan.

Taliban leaders said girls should not go to school. Malala's father was the principal of her school for girls. He encouraged his daughter to tell the world about the difficult days under Taliban rule. So Malala wrote a blog. It first appeared in 2009 in both her native Urdu and in English on British Broadcasting Corporation (BBC) websites. She used the name Gul Makai so that no one would know who was really writing the blog.

"I was getting ready for school," Malala wrote on her blog, "when I remembered that our principal had told us not to wear uniforms—and come to school wearing normal clothes instead."

So Malala dressed in her favorite color, pink, and other girls wore bright colors too. But when they arrived at school, "during the morning assembly we were told not to wear colorful clothes as the Taliban would object to it," Malala wrote.

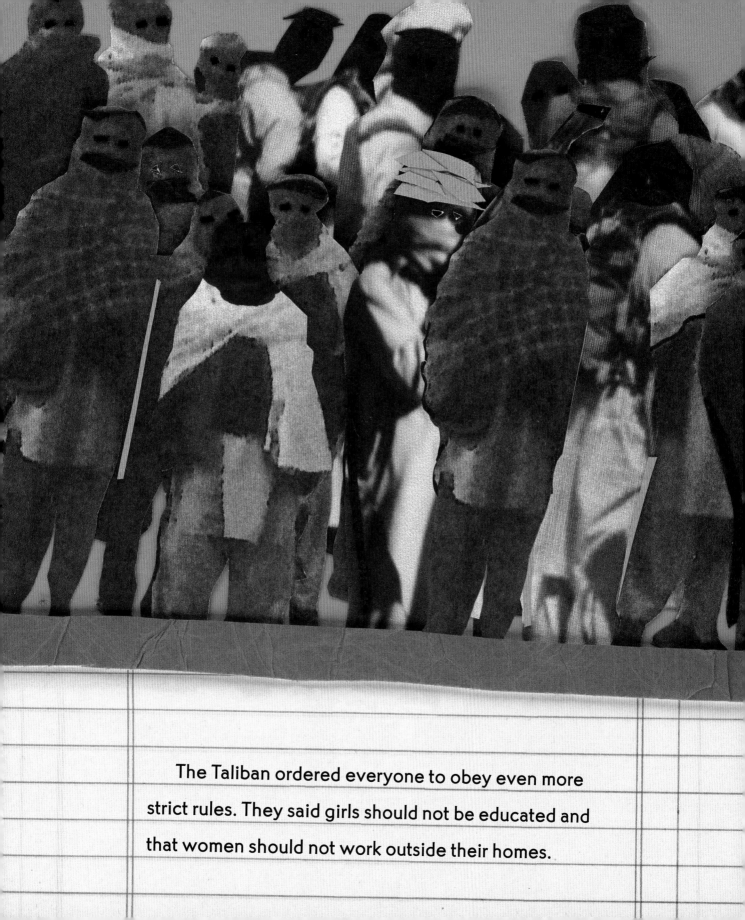

The Taliban ordered everyone to obey even more
strict rules. They said girls should not be educated and
that women should not work outside their homes.

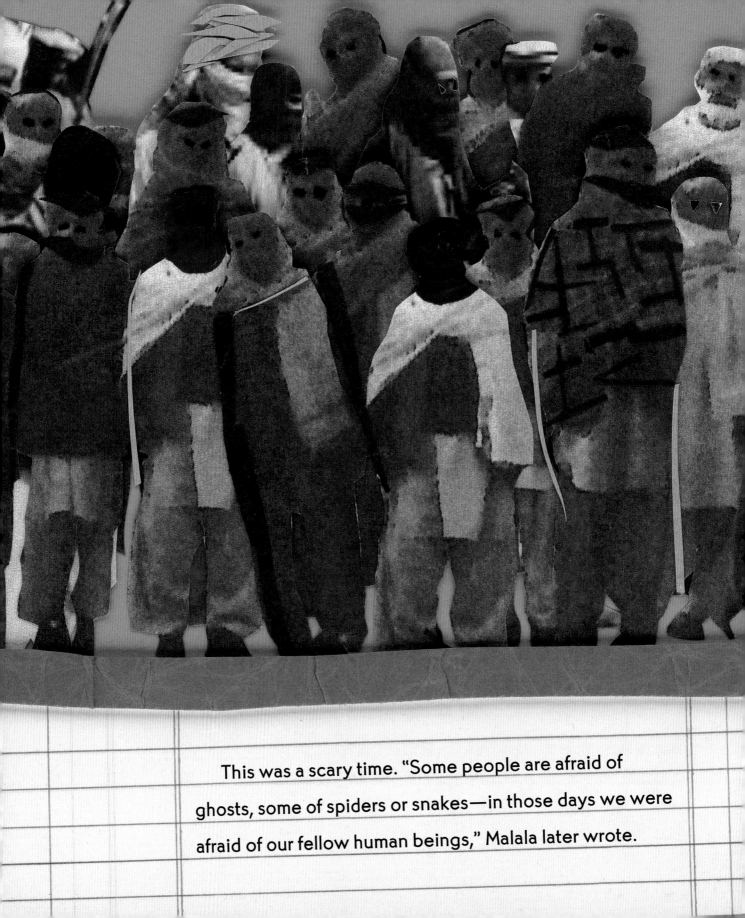

This was a scary time. "Some people are afraid of ghosts, some of spiders or snakes—in those days we were afraid of our fellow human beings," Malala later wrote.

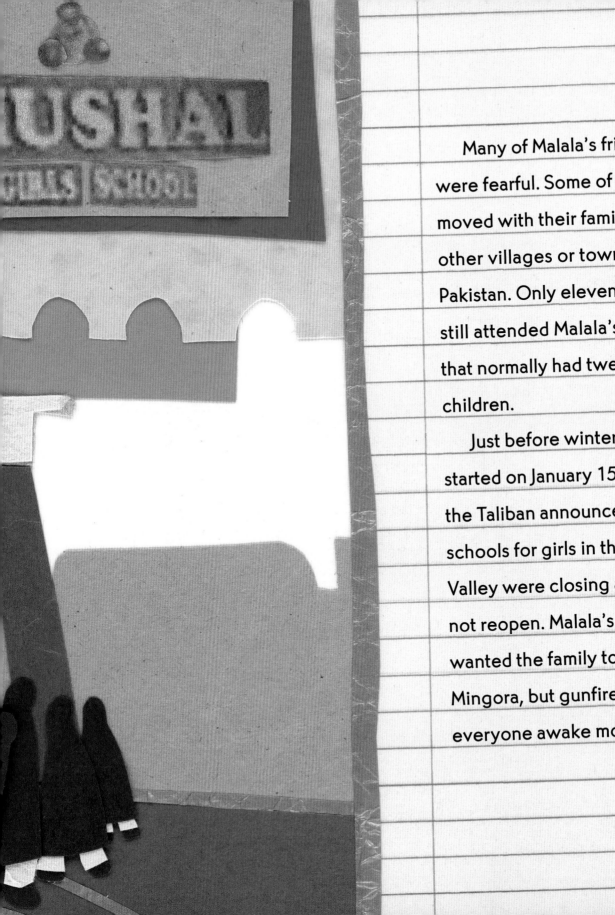

Many of Malala's friends were fearful. Some of them moved with their families to other villages or towns in Pakistan. Only eleven students still attended Malala's class that normally had twenty-seven children.

Just before winter vacation started on January 15, 2009, the Taliban announced that all schools for girls in the Swat Valley were closing and would not reopen. Malala's father wanted the family to stay in Mingora, but gunfire kept everyone awake most nights.

That spring, when Pakistan's army began fighting the Taliban, Malala and her family left the Swat Valley.

Malala packed a school bag with a few books and papers and some clothes. "Leaving the valley was harder than anything I had done before," Malala later wrote. "I stood on our roof looking at the mountains, at the alleys where we used to play. . . . I tried to memorize every detail in case I never saw my home again."

Finally Malala, her mother, and her brothers arrived in the village of Shangla. Malala's father had grown up in Shangla, and he still had relatives and friends there. The trip usually took a few hours by car. This time it took two days. An army officer almost stopped them. They had to walk the last fifteen miles carrying all their things.

By summer the fighting was over, and Malala and her family returned to Migora. The destruction made them weep. Their house was in chaos. But the books and notebooks in Malala's room had not been touched!

Malala's father's school opened again, but many other schools had been destroyed.

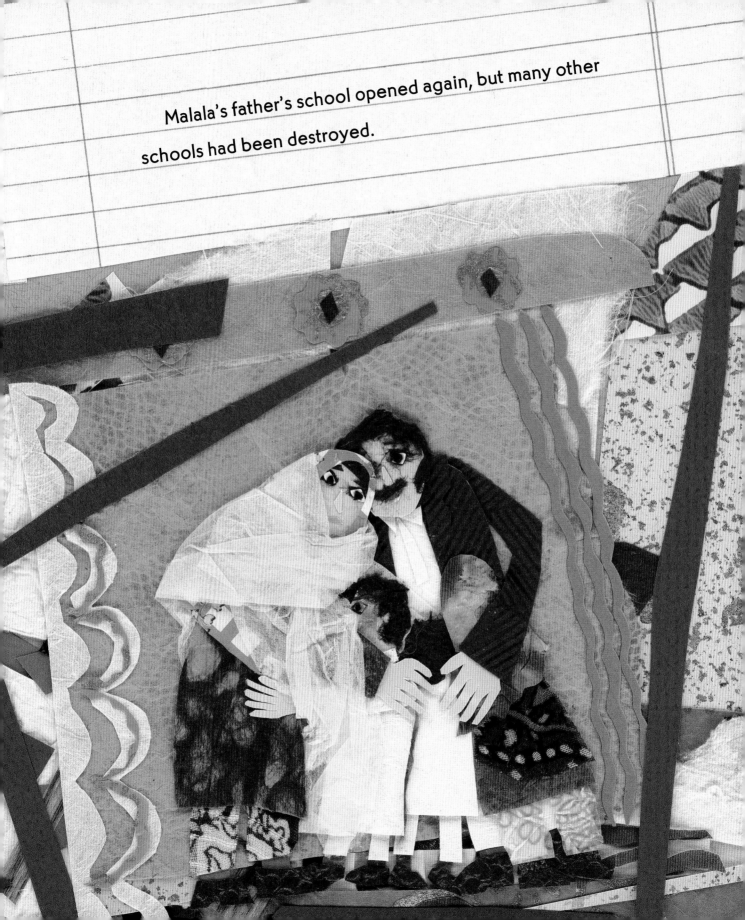

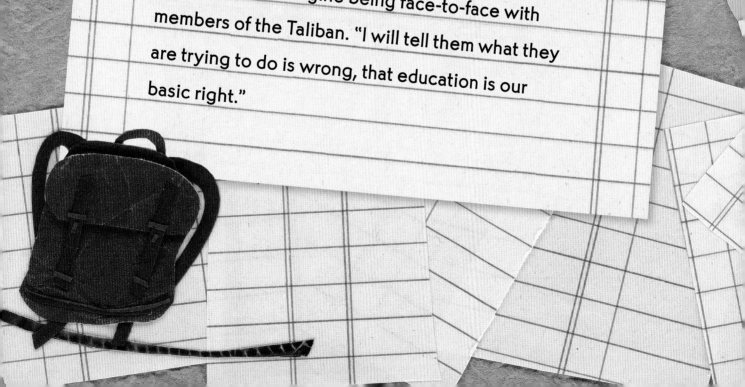

Malala was sad and angry. She began speaking out to everyone who would listen, and she did not hide her name anymore. Malala wanted to prove that peaceful words have power over violence. For her courage, Malala won Pakistan's first National Youth Peace Prize in 2011.

During an interview about the prize for Pakistani television, Malala was asked if she was afraid. Malala said she could imagine being face-to-face with members of the Taliban. "I will tell them what they are trying to do is wrong, that education is our basic right."

On October 9, 2012, when Malala was riding a bus home from school, a man from the Taliban climbed aboard. He shot Malala and two of her friends. Her friends were able to recover in Pakistan, but Malala had been hurt more seriously. She had been shot on the side of her head.

Malala was treated first at two different hospitals in Pakistan. Then she was taken to a hospital in Birmingham, England, that specializes in treating wounded soldiers.

Malala's family and friends feared she might not live.

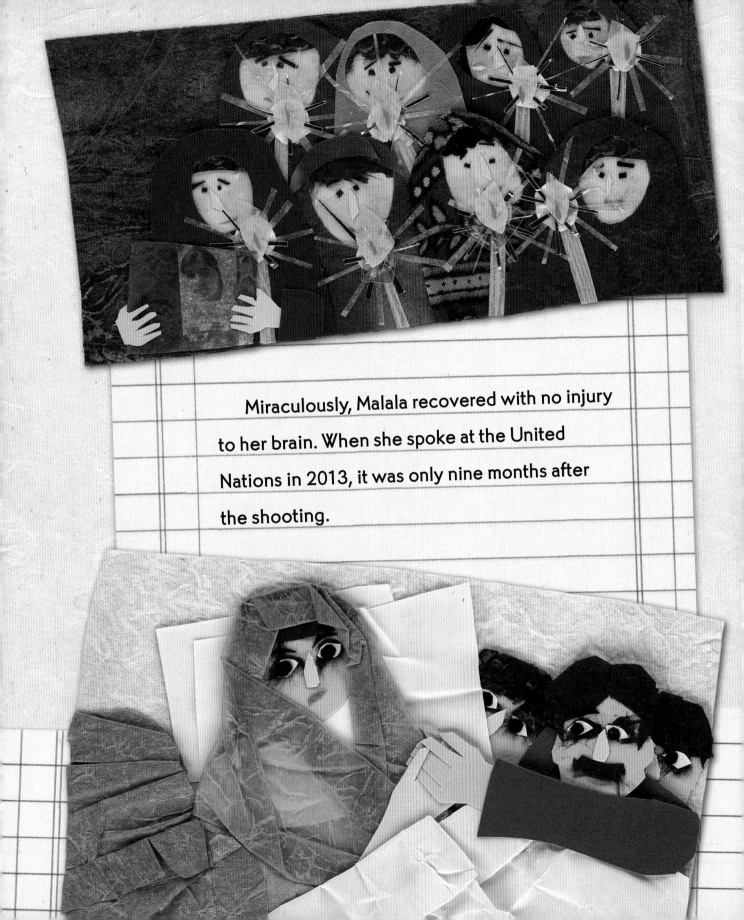

Miraculously, Malala recovered with no injury to her brain. When she spoke at the United Nations in 2013, it was only nine months after the shooting.

"Nothing changed in my life except this: Weakness, fear, and hopelessness died," Malala declared. "Strength, power, and courage [were] born. I am the same Malala. My ambitions are the same. My hopes are the same. My dreams are the same."

After her recovery Malala began attending school in England, where she lived with her family. She continued to share her hopes and words. People around the world answered with rallies, prayer vigils, and marches, often singing "I am Malala."

In October 2013, Malala and her father formed the Malala Fund. The fund works to give girls hope for an education and a better life. On the fund's website it says, "If one educated girl can change the world, imagine what 130 million girls could do."

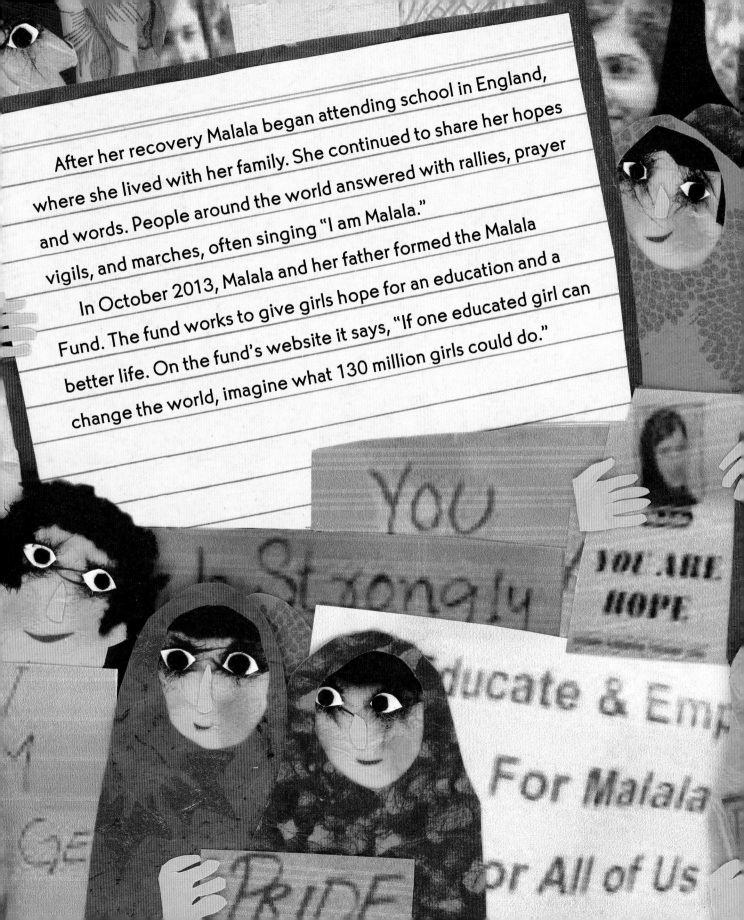

In 2014, at the age of seventeen, Malala became the youngest person to win the Nobel Peace Prize. She received the award along with Kailash Satyarthi. Satyarthi is from India. He has worked for many years to allow children to go to school instead of being forced to work.

When she accepted the Nobel Prize, Malala said, "This award is not just for me. It is for those forgotten children who want education. It is for those frightened children who want peace. It is for those voiceless children who want change."

Before Malala began her studies at the University of Oxford in England in 2017, she traveled the globe on a journey she called her Girl Power Trip. She met girls everywhere who were being denied an education. She talked with world leaders and asked them to take action.

When she returned, Malala continued to lead the fight for all children in every country to go to school in peace. She wants every girl and boy to stand up and speak out for the millions of children worldwide who are not yet able to attend school.

Pink may no longer be her favorite color, but Malala Yousafzai is still a warrior with words. As she said at the United Nations in 2013, "Let us pick up our books and pens. . . . One child, one teacher, one pen, and one book can change the world."

## PAKISTAN

The territories that are now Afghanistan, Pakistan, and India were once part of the British Empire. The British Parliament voted to end British control over India in 1947. Muhammad Ali Jinnah, a politician and lawyer, united Muslims in India and worked hard to create an independent homeland for his people. Later in 1947, the Islamic Republic of Pakistan was established as a majority Muslim country, and the Republic of India became a majority Hindu country.

At first Pakistan consisted of two areas, West Pakistan and East Pakistan, with India in the middle. There have been several wars between India and Pakistan, usually because of disagreements about borders. In 1971, as a result of another devastating war, East Pakistan became the independent nation of Bangladesh. West Pakistan then became known simply as Pakistan.

Malala Yousafzai and her family are Pashtun. Pashtuns are a mainly Muslim people who belong to about sixty different tribes living in Pakistan and Afghanistan.

## THE TALIBAN

*Talib* is the word for "student" in Arabic and Pashto, the language spoken by Pashtuns. The Taliban are Pashtuns who come from religious schools that teach a very strict, conservative form of Islam. Along with other groups, the Taliban fought to end control of Afghanistan by the former Soviet Union (now Russia). The conflict lasted from 1979 until 1996, when the Taliban took power in Afghanistan. They also wanted to control the parts of Pakistan where Pashtun Muslims lived, especially northern areas such as the Swat Valley.

In July 2009, the Pakistani Army announced that it had defeated the Taliban in Swat. People returned to Mingora and the Swat Valley. As of 2016, tourists were also returning to the valley to vacation and ski, but Pakistani soldiers still operate checkpoints going into and out of the area. There has also been some progress for girls and women. Swat has its first woman lawyer, and there is a women's-only *jirga*, a traditional decision-making assembly of leaders, to help ensure justice for girls and women.

In spite of these developments, the Taliban remain in the Swat Valley and in other areas of Pakistan and Afghanistan.

## THE MALALA FUND

The Malala Fund was founded in 2013 by Malala and her father, Ziauddin Yousafzai. Since then the fund has gained worldwide support from people of all ages and backgrounds.

The fund works "for a world where every girl can learn and lead without fear." The first director of the fund was Shiza Shahid, another young Pakistani woman. She graduated from Stanford University in the United States and once organized a summer camp for Malala and other girls in the Swat Valley. Shiza has said, "Teaching someone you know who isn't going to school or helping someone who is suffering or focusing your career on what you believe will make a difference in the future. We all have ways to make a difference."

On the Malala Fund's website it says that 130 million girls were out of school in 2017. One way the fund is trying to improve this situation is through its Gulmakai Network. It is named after Gul Makai, the name Malala used when she blogged for the BBC in 2009. The network supports and gives grants of money to "Gulmakai champions," people who are working hard to help more girls go to high school in developing countries around the world. Gulalai Ismail was one of the first Gulmakai champions. When she was sixteen years old, she co-founded Aware Girls with her sister. Gulalai used her grant to strengthen girls' leadership skills, research barriers to girls' education, and advocate for changes to help make twelve years of schooling available to all girls in Pakistan.

Another way the Malala Fund is helping girls' education is through the building of schools. In 2018, a new school for girls opened in the Shangla district of Pakistan. The school building as well as books, students' uniforms, and teachers' salaries were paid for with Malala's Nobel Peace Prize money.

Also in 2018, the computer company Apple Inc. became the Malala Fund's first corporate partner. With Apple's support, the fund will double the number of grants given through the Gulmakai Network. The partnership will also help the Malala Fund expand its efforts to India and Latin America by providing enough financing for 100,000 girls to go to high school.

Malala Yousafzai

## TAKING ACTION

Do you remember being excited the first time you had your own backpack for school or climbed onto a school bus? Too many children in the world never have a chance to know that excitement.

About 263 million children and teenagers are not in school around the world, according to the United Nations Educational, Scientific and Cultural Organization (UNESCO). These are the children Malala and the Malala Fund are helping. Many other organizations, such as those listed below, are also working to help girls and boys get to school, and several offer opportunities for you to get involved. Some of the organizations were even started by young people!

The **Swat Relief Initiative (SRI)** works in the Swat Valley of Pakistan to improve health, educational, environmental, and economic opportunities for children and women. It is led by Zebu Jilani, granddaughter of the last ruler of Swat before it became a province of Pakistan. The SRI's goal is to place 20,000 children who are not in school in classes by the year 2020.

Ghazala Khan and Saima Sherin are middle school girls in Pakistan's Swat Valley. They live in the town of Islampur, a few miles from Malala's home in Mingora. Ghazala and Saima attend a girls' school run by the SRI, which provides them with free uniforms, books, and transportation so they are able to keep going to school. Ghazala says, "I am hopeful that this school will change my future and my school fellows' future. And we will change our village's future."

The **Youth Activism Project**, founded in 1992, supports community action led by young people. Anika Manzoor, who was also involved with School Girls Unite (see the next section), is now the executive director of this organization. Anika says she was inspired to take action by Malala's "eloquence, her bravery, and her steadfast commitment to education in the face of fire." The Youth Activism Project promotes leadership and encourages groups led by young people of all ages in the United States and abroad to work together, locally and globally, to find solutions to problems about which they care deeply.

**School Girls Unite (SGU)** is an initiative of the Youth Activism Project. It was started in 2004 by middle school girls in Maryland who talked with young women from the African country of Mali about the unfair treatment of girls in many poor countries. SGU raises money to provide scholarships for girls in Mali to attend school. To encourage other girls to take action, SGU has created two guides: *Girls Gone Activist!* and *The Activist Gameplan*. SGU members also participated in the worldwide effort to urge the United Nations to establish the International Day of the Girl, which is now celebrated every year on October 11.

**Theirworld** is an organization that works to create "a brighter future for every child" around the world. Members work in underdeveloped countries to save the lives of babies and improve their health. They also help provide educational opportunities for refugee children.

**Girl Up**, a United Nations Foundation campaign, started in 2010 as a movement to offer girls in the United States a chance to become world leaders. It has since taken on an international focus. Girl Up provides money to programs in developing countries that support the education, health, safety, and leadership efforts of girls.

# QUOTATION SOURCES

back cover: "Education is . . . basic right." Malala Yousafzai, quoted in Basharat Peer, "The Girl Who Wanted to Go to School." *The New Yorker*, October 10, 2012. https://www.newyorker.com/news/news-desk/the-girl-who-wanted-to-go-to-school.

page 6: "We will . . . our voice." Malala Yousafzai, speech at the Youth Takeover of the United Nations, July 12, 2013. Theirworld. https://theirworld.org/explainers/malala-yousafzais-speech-at-the-youth-takeover-of-the-united-nations.
"Our words . . . the world." Ibid.

page 12: "I was . . . clothes instead." Malala Yousafzai, BBC blog entry, Monday, January 5, 2009. The Malala Yousafzai Blog & Story. http://www.malala-yousafzai.com/2012/10/Malala-Diary-for-BBC.html.
"during the . . . object to it." Ibid.

page 15: "Some people . . . human beings." Malala Yousafzai, in *I Am Malala: The Girl Who Stood Up for Education and Was Shot by the Taliban* (New York: Little, Brown and Company, 2013), p. 166.

page 18: "Leaving the. . . done before." Ibid, p. 176.
"I stood . . . home again." Malala Yousafzai, in *I Am Malala: How One Girl Stood Up for Education and Changed the World* (New York: Little, Brown and Company, 2014), p. 96.

page 22: "I will . . . basic right." Malala Yousafzai, quoted in Basharat Peer, "The Girl Who Wanted to Go to School." *The New Yorker*, October 10, 2012. https://www.newyorker.com/news/news-desk/the-girl-who-wanted-to-go-to-school.

page 27: "Nothing changed . . . the same." Malala Yousafzai, speech at the Youth Takeover of the United Nations, July 12, 2013. Theirworld. https://theirworld.org/explainers/malala-yousafzais-speech-at-the-youth-takeover-of-the-united-nations.

page 28: "If one . . . could do." Malala Yousafzai, Malala Fund website, December 14, 2017. https://blog.malala.org/ive-heard-from-girls-now-i-want-you-to-hear-from-them-too-61e1c5b7dba3.

page 30: "This award . . . want change." Malala Yousafzai, Nobel Lecture, December 10, 2014. Nobelprize.org. https://www.nobelprize.org/nobel_prizes/peace/laureates/2014/yousafzai-lecture_en.html.

page 32: "Let us . . . the world." Malala Yousafzai, speech at the Youth Takeover of the United Nations, July 12, 2013. Theirworld. https://theirworld.org/explainers/malala-yousafzais-speech-at-the-youth-takeover-of-the-united-nations.

page 36: "for a world . . . without fear." Malala Fund website. https://www.malala.org/about.
"Teaching someone . . . a difference." Shiza Shahid, Voice of America interview with the author, 2013.

page 38: "I am hopeful . . . village's future." Ghazala Khan, letter to the author, October 16, 2017.
"eloquence, her . . . face of fire." Anika Manzoor, interview with the author, 2018.

page 39: "a brighter . . . every child." Theirworld website. https://theirworld.org.

# AUTHOR'S SOURCES

Ali, Lehaz. "Fragile Peace at Girls' School Malala Built in Pakistan." France 24, March 30, 2018. http://www.france24.com/en/20180330-fragile-peace-girls-school-malala-built-pakistan.

Aware Girls: Working Towards Gender Equality and Peace. http://www.awaregirls.org.

Conelley, Joanne, Gaëlle Dessus, Anna Diarra, et al., eds. *Girls Gone Activist! Youth Activism Project*, School Girls Unite, 2009. https://schoolgirlsunite.files.wordpress.com/2016/06/ebook-girlsgoneactivist.pdf.

Ellick, Adam B. and Irfan Ashraf. "Class Dismissed: The Death of Female Education." Documentary. *The New York Times*, 2009. https://www.youtube.com/watch?v=3ZG5IdnJn4I.

Girl Up. https://girlup.org.

Ismail, Gulalai. Email correspondence with the author, 2018.

Jilani, Zebu. Email and phone conversations with the author, 2017 and 2018.

Malala Fund. https://www.malala.org.

"Malala—Shot for Going to School." Interview with Malala Yousafzai. BBC Outlook, January 2012. http://www.bbc.co.uk/programmes/p00ys51s.

"Malala Yousafzai Full Diary for BBC (Gul Makai)." The Malala Yousafzai Blog & Story, October 27, 2012. http://www.malala-yousafzai.com/2012/10/Malala-Diary-for-BBC.html.

Malala Yousafzai—Nobel Lecture. Nobelprize.org, December 10, 2014. https://www.nobelprize.org/nobel_prizes/peace/laureates/2014/yousafzai-lecture_en.html.

"Malala Yousafzai: Portrait of the girl blogger." BBC News Magazine, October 10, 2012. http://www.bbc.com/news/magazine-19899540.

Manzoor, Anika. Interview with the author, 2018.

"Pakistan Country Profile." BBC News, August 2, 2017. http://www.bbc.com/news/world-south-asia-12965779.

Peer, Basharat. "The Girl Who Wanted to Go to School." *The New Yorker*, October 10, 2012. https://www.newyorker.com/news/news-desk/the-girl-who-wanted-to-go-to-school.

School Girls Unite. https://schoolgirlsunite.org.

Shahid, Shiza. Voice of America interview with the author, 2013.

Siddiqui, Taha, Jasmin Lavoie, Shahzaib Eahlah, and Aftab Ahmed. "Pakistan's Swat Valley striving to return to its former glory." France 24, February 10, 2017. http://www.france24.com/en/20170210-video-revisited-pakistan-swat-valley-taliban-former-glory.

Swat Relief Initiative. http://swatreliefinitiative.org/index.html.

Theirworld. https://theirworld.org.

"263 Million Children and Youth Are Out of School." UNESCO Institute for Statistics, July 15, 2016. http://uis.unesco.org/en/news/263-million-children-and-youth-are-out-school.

Yousafzai, Malala. "Diary of a Pakistani Schoolgirl." BBC News, January—March 2009. http://news.bbc.co.uk/2/hi/south_asia/7834402.stm.

———."Speech at the Youth Takeover of the United Nations." Theirworld. https://theirworld.org/explainers/malala-yousafzais-speech-at-the-youth-takeover-of-the-united-nations.

———, with Christina Lamb. *I Am Malala: The Girl Who Stood Up for Education and Was Shot by the Taliban*. New York: Little, Brown and Company, 2013.

———, with Patricia McCormick. *I Am Malala: How One Girl Stood Up for Education and Changed the World* (Young Readers Edition). New York: Little, Brown and Company, 2014.

Youth Activism Project. http://youthactivism-project.org.